Weekly Planner
2016

Copyright © 2014

Speedy Publishing LLC
40 E. Main St., #1156,
Newark, DE 19711
www.speedypublishing.co

Publisher's Note: This is a work of fiction. Names, characters, places, and incidents are a product of the author's imagination. Locales and public names are sometimes used for atmospheric purposes. Any resemblance to actual people, living or dead, or to businesses, companies, events, institutions, or locales is completely coincidental.

Speedy Publishing LLC©2014

Ordering Information:
Quantity sales. Special discounts are available on quantity purchases by corporations, associations, and others. For details, contact the "Special Sales Department" at the address above.

Weekly Planner 2016 -- 1st ed.
ISBN 978-1-6328794-8-6

Date: ________________________________

Monday

____

____

____

Tuesday

____

____

____

Wednesday

____

____

____

Thursday

____

____

____

Friday

____

____

____

Saturday

____

____

____

Sunday

____

____

____

Date: ______________________________

Monday

Tuesday

Wednesday

Thursday

Friday

Saturday

Sunday

Date: ___________________________

Monday

____
____
____

Tuesday

____
____
____

Wednesday

____
____
____

Thursday

____
____
____

Friday

____
____
____

Saturday

____
____
____

Sunday

____
____
____

Date: ___________________________

Monday

Tuesday

Wednesday

Thursday

Friday

Saturday

Sunday

Date: _______________________________

Monday

____
____
____

Tuesday

____
____
____

Wednesday

____
____
____

Thursday

____
____
____

Friday

____
____
____

Saturday

____
____
____

Sunday

____
____
____

Date: ______________________________

Monday

____
____
____

Tuesday

____
____
____

Wednesday

____
____
____

Thursday

____
____
____

Friday

____
____
____

Saturday

____
____
____

Sunday

____
____
____

Date: ________________________

Monday

Tuesday

Wednesday

Thursday

Friday

Saturday

Sunday

Date: ____________________________

Monday

Tuesday

Wednesday

Thursday

Friday

Saturday

Sunday

Date: _______________________________

Monday

Tuesday

Wednesday

Thursday

Friday

Saturday

Sunday

Date: ___________________________

Monday

____

____

____

Tuesday

____

____

____

Wednesday

____

____

____

Thursday

____

____

____

Friday

____

____

____

Saturday

____

____

____

Sunday

____

____

____

Date: _______________________________

Monday

____

____

____

Tuesday

____

____

____

Wednesday

____

____

____

Thursday

____

____

____

Friday

____

____

____

Saturday

____

____

____

Sunday

____

____

____

Date: ___________________________

Monday

Tuesday

Wednesday

Thursday

Friday

Saturday

Sunday

Date: _______________________________

Monday

____
____
____

Tuesday

____
____
____

Wednesday

____
____
____

Thursday

____
____
____

Friday

____
____
____

Saturday

____
____
____

Sunday

____
____
____

Date: _______________________________

Monday

____
____
____

Tuesday

____
____
____

Wednesday

____
____
____

Thursday

____
____
____

Friday

____
____
____

Saturday

____
____
____

Sunday

____
____
____

Date: ___________________________

Monday

Tuesday

Wednesday

Thursday

Friday

Saturday

Sunday

Date: _______________________________

Monday

____
____
____

Tuesday

____
____
____

Wednesday

____
____
____

Thursday

____
____
____

Friday

____
____
____

Saturday

____
____
____

Sunday

____
____
____

Date: _______________________________

Monday

____

____

____

Tuesday

____

____

____

Wednesday

____

____

____

Thursday

____

____

____

Friday

____

____

____

Saturday

____

____

____

Sunday

____

____

____

Date: _______________________________

Monday

Tuesday

Wednesday

Thursday

Friday

Saturday

Sunday

Date: _______________________________

Monday

____
____
____

Tuesday

____
____
____

Wednesday

____
____
____

Thursday

____
____
____

Friday

____
____
____

Saturday

____
____
____

Sunday

____
____
____

Date: ___________________________

Monday

____

____

____

Tuesday

____

____

____

Wednesday

____

____

____

Thursday

____

____

____

Friday

____

____

____

Saturday

____

____

____

Sunday

____

____

____

Date: _______________________________

Monday

Tuesday

Wednesday

Thursday

Friday

Saturday

Sunday

Date: _________________________________

Monday

____
____
____

Tuesday

____
____
____

Wednesday

____
____
____

Thursday

____
____
____

Friday

____
____
____

Saturday

____
____
____

Sunday

____
____
____

Date: _______________________________

Monday

Tuesday

Wednesday

Thursday

Friday

Saturday

Sunday

Date: ______________________________

Monday

Tuesday

Wednesday

Thursday

Friday

Saturday

Sunday

Date: _______________________________

Monday

____

____

____

Tuesday

____

____

____

Wednesday

____

____

____

Thursday

____

____

____

Friday

____

____

____

Saturday

____

____

____

Sunday

____

____

____

Date: _______________________________

Monday

Tuesday

Wednesday

Thursday

Friday

Saturday

Sunday

Date: _______________________________

Monday

____

____

____

Tuesday

____

____

____

Wednesday

____

____

____

Thursday

____

____

____

Friday

____

____

____

Saturday

____

____

____

Sunday

____

____

____

Date: _______________________________

Monday

____

____

____

Tuesday

____

____

____

Wednesday

____

____

____

Thursday

____

____

____

Friday

____

____

____

Saturday

____

____

____

Sunday

____

____

____

Date: _______________________________

Monday

____
____
____

Tuesday

____
____
____

Wednesday

____
____
____

Thursday

____
____
____

Friday

____
____
____

Saturday

____
____
____

Sunday

____
____
____

Date: _______________________________

Monday

____
____
____

Tuesday

____
____
____

Wednesday

____
____
____

Thursday

____
____
____

Friday

____
____
____

Saturday

____
____
____

Sunday

____
____
____

Date: _______________________________

Monday

Tuesday

Wednesday

Thursday

Friday

Saturday

Sunday

Date: ___________________________

Monday

____

____

____

Tuesday

____

____

____

Wednesday

____

____

____

Thursday

____

____

____

Friday

____

____

____

Saturday

____

____

____

Sunday

____

____

____

Date: _______________________________

Monday

____

____

____

Tuesday

____

____

____

Wednesday

____

____

____

Thursday

____

____

____

Friday

____

____

____

Saturday

____

____

____

Sunday

____

____

____

Date: _______________________________

Monday

Tuesday

Wednesday

Thursday

Friday

Saturday

Sunday

Date: _______________________________

Monday

____

____

____

Tuesday

____

____

____

Wednesday

____

____

____

Thursday

____

____

____

Friday

____

____

____

Saturday

____

____

____

Sunday

____

____

____

Date: ______________________________

Monday

Tuesday

Wednesday

Thursday

Friday

Saturday

Sunday

Date: _______________________________

Monday

____
____
____

Tuesday

____
____
____

Wednesday

____
____
____

Thursday

____
____
____

Friday

____
____
____

Saturday

____
____
____

Sunday

____
____
____

Date: _______________________________

Monday

Tuesday

Wednesday

Thursday

Friday

Saturday

Sunday

Date: ___________________________

Monday

Tuesday

Wednesday

Thursday

Friday

Saturday

Sunday

Date: _______________________________

Monday

Tuesday

Wednesday

Thursday

Friday

Saturday

Sunday

Date: _______________________________

Monday

____

____

____

Tuesday

____

____

____

Wednesday

____

____

____

Thursday

____

____

____

Friday

____

____

____

Saturday

____

____

____

Sunday

____

____

____

Date: _______________________________

Monday

____
____
____

Tuesday

____
____
____

Wednesday

____
____
____

Thursday

____
____
____

Friday

____
____
____

Saturday

____
____
____

Sunday

____
____
____

Date: ___________________________

Monday

Tuesday

Wednesday

Thursday

Friday

Saturday

Sunday

Note:

Note:

Note:

Note:

Note: